TWO VOICES

A collection of art and poetry

By **Irene E. Peña** and **Amado M. Peña, Jr.**

 KIVA
PUBLISHING, INC.

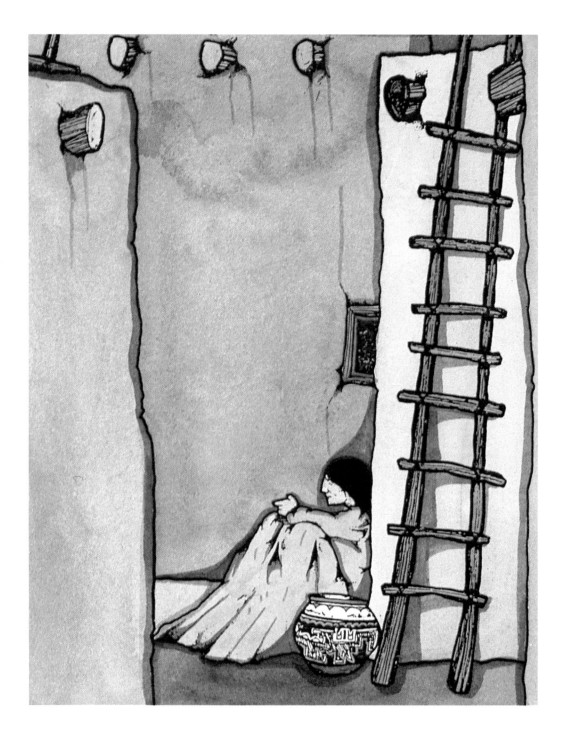

Taos

Housetops seem to sway
to the cool, crisp rhythm
of the morning.
Even the sun is trying to be
gentle this morning.
Evergreens perfectly clustered
dress the mountains
as if making sure
nothing is out of place...
preparing for a perfect day.

Rain in Tesuque

Gray clouds stretch
their arms across the sky,
rumbling as they move,
determined to hide
the transparency of the summer sky
as they announce
the coming of an afternoon shower.

Dad

You never told
unimportant stories,
just filled
my memory
so that on a day
such as today
I would remember you
and be glad I paid attention.

At the Pueblo

Old man with braided hair
your face tells the story
of a hard life
already half gone.

You sit with shoulders uncovered
unmoved by the long line of cars,
by the noisy voices of tourists
ready to invade your life again.

Mother

I didn't suffer
like my mother
in silence and alone.
All that pain... for what,
I wondered,
all these years.

First Snow

The winter snow
seems angry,
as she blows relentlessly
over roof tops,
old cars,
and a spotted pup
trying to make it across the street.
She has ravaged us enough...
tomorrow the sun will take revenge.

January 23, 2001

Once the eagle flew
high above the flowing
waters of the river
where I lived,
and as the sun
smiled on the earth
the spirit of my father—
the one I loved—
gave up
the dreams and hopes,
to fly high
with that eagle
to the mountains
where they now rest.

Just Thinking

I have no special love
for certain days
but rainy ones
make me stop and sit
and think those thoughts
like how timidly the rain
falls on the geraniums
and on Dad's rosebushes
that he fondly planted
on those days when he was
stronger than the sun.
It's the rainy days,
blue and gray
that make me stop and sit
and think those thoughts…
Then the rain stops
and I understand
the time was right.

Taos Revisited

Blue-gray skies hover
over rustic mountain ranges.
Sangre de Cristo mountains
watch and protect
this sleepy town.
Winding curves
keep cars from passing.
Mountains eroded by time
stand so proud,
dressed by piñones,
speckled with moss-covered rocks.
The brook scurries below
as if she had somewhere important to go,
someone important to see.

Stella

Your life hung
on empty walls
of people's minds.
For so long your sad eyes
watched this world
spin so fast
as you desperately
cried out.
We heard
but did not listen.
Then one night
you set yourself free
and left us all behind
to wonder why we didn't
or wouldn't
understand.

Amado

My mind has just taken a journey
back to that dusty, unpaved street
and green house where you and I
lived with Guelo, remember?
You spent so much time
under those naranjos in the back yard
making up all kinds of battles...
I always wondered which side won.
You made noises that sounded
like miniature bombs falling,
and those plastic toy soldiers
never seemed to mind dirt
spewing all over them and you.
But when the real battles came
you were not here,
and I faced them alone,
wishing I had practiced
with you in the back yard.

The Day We Met

We met
one afternoon
as the sun
was about to set.

Then Fall came
and stayed,
and so did you.

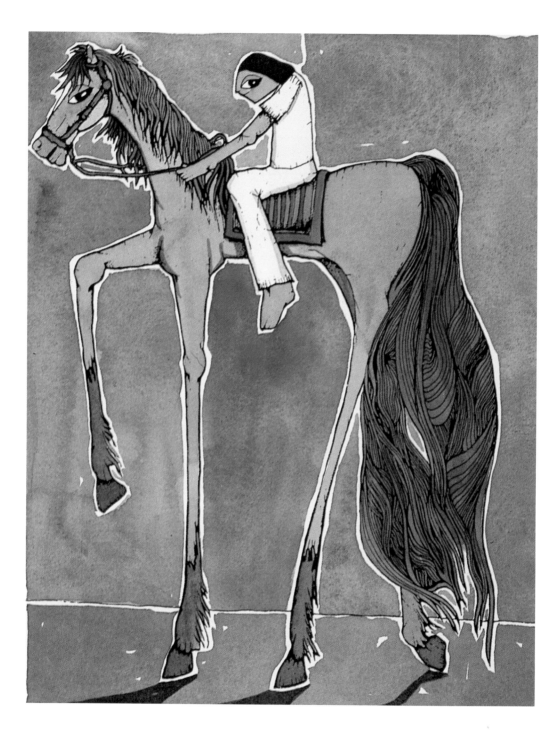

Once a Warrior

Faces and spirits
buried deep in undisturbed white snow,
the hopes of a young warrior
now only faint sounds.
His dreams decided
to cross the river
to where the white man lives.
There they withered
and they, too,
died an undignified death.

Rubin Rose

I boxed memories
of conversations
as one folds old papers
that need to be saved
and placed in drawers
for safekeeping,
so that on rainy June afternoons
like this
I can try to understand
that you were carried
by the wind
to be free.

Untitled

Some day I hope to awaken
as Summer is trying
to rush Fall
into place
and realize
that it was all right
to live in your world
even if it was
just for a while.

Brother and sister, Amado and Irene Pena both left home in Laredo, Texas after high school, to further their education, then set off to form lives with careers and families. Amado's artistic talents were recognized by those around him at an early age. Irene, even before she could write her name, was telling elaborate versions of classical Spanish fairy tales. Amado's talents led him to an artistic career, as both a painter and a master printer, while Irene embarked on a teaching career.

After sixteen years of teaching in Corpus Christi, Laredo, and Austin, Irene took a hiatus from the classroom and joined Amado in his business of art production, marketing and sales in Austin, Texas. These years of working together brought them closer, forging a bond that eventually led to the assembling of *Two Voices*, uniting two art forms as a single heart.

Amado has viewed the Southwest landscape in awe of its beauty and captured its vibrancy with the colors of his brush. Metaphors are Irene's brush, giving life to the mountains, the sky, and the rain.